Modeling with Polymer Clay

by David Kracov

For my Mother and Father—
Thank you for paving the way for my future
and giving me the confidence and guidance
to create my own path.

Walter Foster Publishing, Inc.
23062 La Cadena Drive
Laguna Hills, CA 92653
www.walterfoster.com

Contents

Introduction

For years modeling with polymer clay was considered a mere hobby or craft. It was, and still is, perfect for vases, photo frames, candleholders, baubles, and bangles. But there are other uses for polymer clay beyond the realm of refrigerator magnets and pencil holders. It's time to take polymer clay sculpting to new levels of creativity, and I'm going to show you how.

Why do I use polymer clay rather than traditional clays? The answer is simple—polymer clay is clean and easy to use (perfect for the beginner), and at the same time, it allows the more experienced sculptor the ability to add the finest of details. Unlike modeling clays and oil-based clays, it comes in many colors and can be baked immediately to be permanently hard. There are no long, drawn-out drying periods, no firing in a kiln, no blowing up in the kiln because there were air bubbles in the clay . . . now you see why I like it!

Are there any rules you should be aware of or anything you need before you try your hand at the projects in this book? Yes. Over the years I've learned that, when it comes to creating art, there are no rules; and a budding artist needs only imagination and time. So set aside a little time, shift into creative mode, and let's have some fun sculpting with polymer clay!

Get Ready!

Using Animation Techniques to Sculpt

Some time ago when I was working as an animator at a big animation studio, I was given my first block of polymer clay by the artist who sculpted the maquettes (statues of animated characters we animators use as drawing references). I could not wait to get home that evening and begin creating. Not knowing anything about sculpting, I was not sure where or how to start, but after a few hours of experimenting, I was hooked. My first sculpture was a self-portrait—not a good one, but it didn't matter. It was *my* creation based on *my* imagination. That was when I realized that sculpting and animation follow similar paths.

Designing a Sculpture
First I make a sketch of the subject I want to sculpt, breaking it down into simple shapes: circles, ovals, and rectangles. These are my working drawings for Rupert the Dragon and Wendell the Rhino.

As an animator, I begin my designs by breaking the character down into geometric shapes—an egg for the head, an hourglass for the body, elongated ovals for the arms and legs, and circles for the hands. On a whim, I decided to try this same technique three-dimensionally. It worked! First I practiced creating geometric shapes with the clay—rolling a perfectly smooth ball and forming an even square. Once I felt comfortable with this, I went through my clipping file to find photos of animals I wanted to sculpt. I would lay a piece of tracing paper over the photo and trace the animal's features with geometric shapes. Using the drawing as a guide, I began to sculpt my character starting with the basic shapes and then adding the details. This is where another aspect of animation became useful. When designing humorous characters, whether human or animal, it is helpful to think in terms of caricature.

A *caricature* is a design of a person, animal, or object that is exaggerated in some form. For example, rabbits have long ears, so the sculpture would be designed with exaggerated ears. A caricature of Jimmy Durante would be sculpted with an oversized nose, and so on. As you read, notice that all the projects in this book have some form of overemphasis of the characters' features.

Basic Tools

Only a few basic tools are needed to make the projects in this book, and all of the supplies can be purchased at any art supply store or craft and hobby shop. Also, keep in mind that anything you put in your hand can be used as a sculpting tool. As most sculptors use the "carving away" process of sculpting, many of the sculpting tools available at hobby shops and art supply stores serve those needs. However, I will be teaching the "building up" process of sculpting in which clay is added rather than taken away. As you become comfortable with the tools in the following list, you can begin to experiment with all kinds of objects.

- Prēmo!Sculpey™ brand polymer clay
- utility knife and #11 blades
- wood-handled stylus (If you cannot find one, a new nail taped or glued to a wood handle makes a great substitute.)
- mat knife with heavy-duty snap-off blades
- pasta maker (A marble or metal rolling pin will work just as well, but do not use a wooden rolling pin, because the clay will stick to the surface.)
- tweezers (These are used for detailing.)
- 1/8" wood dowels (These are used for support in larger sculptures where toothpicks are too small.)
- instant glue, preferably cyanoacrylate adhesive brands (please refer to the section on gluing, page 7)
- combo circle template
- wood block—any hard wood at least 1" thick and big enough to hold your sculpture
- large round or sandwich toothpicks

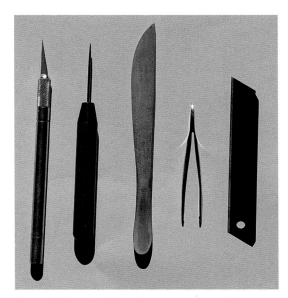

Essential Tools A utility knife, stylus, wooden sculpting tool, tweezers, and mat knife with snap-off blades are some of the tools of the trade.

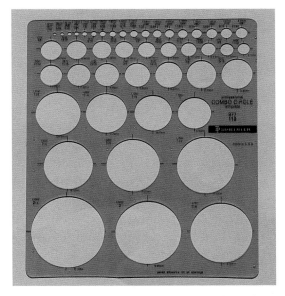

Combo Circle Template Not too many people can draw a perfect circle, let alone cut one from clay. This one has circles from 1/16" to 1-7/8" in diameter.

Properties of Prēmo! Sculpey™ Clay

Prēmo!Sculpey™ brand polymer clay will be used throughout this book (I'll be referring to it from now on as Premo). When kneading Premo before you begin to model, you will notice

that it quickly softens to a workable consistency. In its unbaked state, Premo has a "memory." This means that whatever you sculpt will keep its shape and not sag, as many other polymer clays will do. When baked, Premo has the consistency of hard plastic and is extremely durable. Even the thinnest part of your sculpture will have some "give," allowing it to absorb slight bumps and shocks. Premo's colors do not lose their vibrancy even when baked, and they have a matte, antiqued look to them.

Premo comes in 32 colors and assorted sizes. You can also custom-blend colors by combining two or more colors of clay and kneading thoroughly until uniform.

Ovens and Baking Temperatures

Because we will be working on a small scale, either gas or electric ovens are recommended. Although some sculptors use a toaster oven for baking small parts, I would not recommend it. They are unreliable, and there is a high risk of burning the sculpture.

Although oven temperatures vary, a safe temperature to bake Premo is 275°. Preheat the oven for at least 15 minutes, and then bake the clay. The rule of thumb is, for each 1/4" thickness of clay, bake for a minimum of 20 minutes. You'll find that the times vary greatly, but as you progress you'll get a better sense for the various sizes of sculptures and their appropriate baking times.

Baking Surfaces

A block of hard wood is an ideal baking surface on which to rest your sculpture. Poplar and ash are good woods to use (get a block that is at least 1" thick) and can be purchased at your local hardware store. If you're worried about the wood catching fire in the oven—don't. It won't be left in the oven long enough to burn. You need a thick block of wood because you'll be drilling holes in it to hold the wood dowels that will support your sculpture. One thing to keep in mind is that the part of the sculpture that touches the wood will not bake as quickly as the rest of the sculpture. About halfway through baking, the sculpture will have to be laid on its side to allow the underside to bake.

Another great baking surface is a pizza stone, which can be purchased at most department stores. Preheat the oven with the pizza stone on the lowest rack for a minimum of 30 minutes, allowing the stone to heat all the way through. The advantage to using a pizza stone is that all parts of the sculpture bake evenly, so you don't have to turn the sculpture on its side.

Knowing When the Sculpture Has Fully Baked

The first rule of baking polymer clay is that when you believe the sculpture has fully baked, turn the oven off, and leave the sculpture in the oven. There are two reasons for allowing the clay to cool off in the oven. First, the sculpture is extremely hot when baked, and when going from a hot oven to cool air, tiny cracks and splinters will form. Second, your sculpture is at its most vulnerable right after baking. If you poke the clay with a fingernail or any pointed object, there is a good chance you'll leave a mark. Let the clay cool for about 15 minutes before you check it. If you lightly squeeze the sculpture and it feels soft, repeat the baking procedure.

As you become more skilled at sculpting and add more detail to your work, you'll find that certain parts of the sculpture finish baking before others do. The best solution to this problem is to cover the thin areas with sheets of clay. For example, when baking a sculpture of a person, place a small sheet of clay over the nose (use the same color clay for the sheet as the part being covered). The covered nose will bake more slowly, keeping it in relation to the rest of the sculpture. Because the sheet of clay covering the nose is small and thin, it will burn extremely fast, but this will not affect the sculpture.

Gluing

When building a sculpture, sometimes it is necessary to sculpt certain parts separately and glue them together after baking. For example, the sculpture of the beaver is posed with a hammer in one hand and a lunchbox in the other. Because the clay is soft and pliable before baking, if the sculpture were baked with the hammer and lunchbox in place, the arms would droop from the weight. To compensate for this, the hands are shaped to hold the objects but baked without them.

Attaching Baked Parts Heavy items, such as this lunchbox, that would deform the sculpture are baked separately and glued on later after they have cooled.

Whenever you feel that the sculpture will become misshapen from the weight of its parts, redesign the sculpture so that the parts in question can be baked separately and attached after baking. This technique should also be used when parts to a sculpture are too flimsy. For example, if you were sculpting a mouse with a long, thin tail, you should shape the tail into the pose you want, bake it separately, and then glue it to the sculpture.

Any type of porous adhering glue can be used with polymer clays. For the best results, I recommend using cyanoacrylate glue or hobby glue. I use one with a gel-like consistency that has a curing time of 10–25 seconds. The long curing time allows you to remove and reposition parts before the glue hardens. Be careful with the faster-curing glues—they're watery and pour very quickly. When gluing parts together, place one small drop per every square inch. Always apply the glue in drops, never in ribbons. Press the parts firmly together and hold for 20 seconds.

Blending

When attaching two parts of a sculpture that are the same color, the blending technique will give you a clean finish. Begin by lining up and attaching the piece to the sculpture. Using a metal stylus (your fingers are too big and clumsy to use on small sculptures), blend in the excess clay of the part that is being attached.

Blending with a Stylus Blending the clay edges gives a smooth, polished finish.

Holding the stylus between your thumb and index finger, roll the tool back and forth over the clay. Try not to pull the clay with the stylus, or your blending will be uneven.

Before attempting this technique on your sculpture, practice with two small pieces of clay. Begin by pressing the pieces of clay together. Then blend the two pieces by rolling the stylus over the seam until it is perfectly smooth.

Forming a Ball, Cube, and Cane

All the projects in this book begin by taking the subject matter and breaking it down into basic geometric shapes: balls (spheres), cubes, and canes (cylinders).

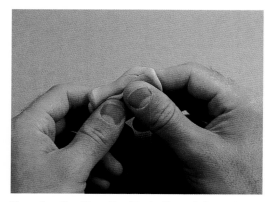

Kneading the Clay Conditioning Premo is fast and easy—just stretch and squash until pliable.

Shaping a Ball A light touch is the secret to forming an even, round ball.

If there is one technique to master, rolling a perfectly even ball is it. First knead the clay until it is soft. Then lightly roll the clay in the palms of your hands. Hold your hands so that one hand is on top of the other. Be careful not to press too firmly, or the ball will be misshapen.

To form a cube, start with a round ball. Then using a flat object such as a small piece of wood, lightly press one side of the ball. Alternating sides, continue to press the sides of the ball until it forms the shape of a cube. If you want to make a square cube, press each side until all are equal. To make a rectangular cube, press one side slightly harder, causing the cube to elongate.

Canes are tubes that can be rolled into various thicknesses and lengths. But unlike the clay "sausages" a child would make using the entire palm, you want to use only the tip of your index finger to the first knuckle. Start with a round ball and gently roll it back and forth, keeping a steady motion, to form an even cane.

Using a Pasta Maker

Most of the projects in this book require the use of extremely thin sheets of clay. You can use a rolling pin, but I find it very difficult to roll out perfectly even clay sheets. Instead, I have discovered that the easiest and quickest way to roll out an even sheet is to use a pasta maker! They're not hard to find—most department stores carry them.

To get the best results from your pasta maker, knead the clay until soft, and remove all air bubbles by pressing firmly. Next roll the clay into a cane, and flatten the cane with your thumb. Then roll the cane through the pasta maker.

Rolling Out Uniform Sheets
I have found that if I turn the handle on the pasta machine quickly, the clay doesn't stick to the rollers.

Most pasta makers have seven thickness settings, #1 being the thickest and #7 being the thinnest. No matter which thickness of clay you ultimately need, always begin with the #1 setting. If you attempt to roll a flattened cane through the #3 setting or thinner, the sheet of clay may get clogged. By progressively rolling the clay through the various settings, the sheet will be smoother with fewer imperfections. If, after rolling the sheet of clay, you find minor imperfections, gently rub them out with the side of your thumb.

Making and Using Templates

Some projects in this book require various shapes to be cut from thin sheets of clay. The best way to make clean, even shapes is to use templates—patterns that provide guidelines for cutting out the shapes. I have provided clothing templates for two of the projects in this book, but you can just as easily make templates yourself.

When making a template, first sketch the basic shape on scrap paper. Test that the shape actually works with your sculpture before you cut out the real one. An index card or any thick, smooth paper is fine for a template. I don't recommend using thin paper because it's hard to remove from the cut clay shape.

After cutting around the template, use the tip of a utility knife to remove the template from the sheet of clay. Be careful not to destroy the shape of the clay you've just cut out.

Basic Sculpting Techniques

It's best to learn by doing. As you follow these steps to sculpt a human, keep in mind that the same techniques will be used to create animals, objects, and anything else your imagination can conceive.

You will need:

- white clay (2 packages)

- black clay (2 packages)

- skin-colored clay (custom-make your own using 2 packages of beige mixed with a little raw sienna)

- blue clay (just a little for the eyes)

- tweezers

- utility knife

- stylus

Head

Despite the wide variation in size and shape of facial features, you can start most sculptures with a simple and generic egg-shaped head.

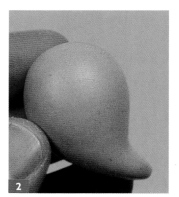

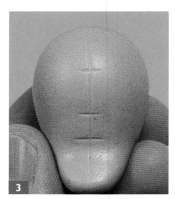

Step One Start by rolling a ball approximately 1-1/8" wide. Turn the ball in your fingers until you create an elongated egg shape.

Step Two Holding the head in one hand, bend the smaller part of the egg shape outward, creating the chin.

Step Three Using a stylus, gently score a line down the center of the face. Next mark where the lips, base of the nose, and eyes will be placed.

Lips

The mouth is easy to form if you apply upper and lower lips separately. Leave the delicate shaping until both are attached.

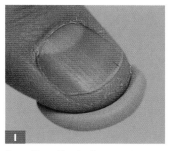

Step One For the lips, start by making a ball approximately 3/8" wide. With your thumb, press down the center of the ball.

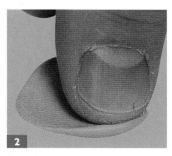

Step Two Roll the tip of your thumb forward, creating a "lip" around the flattened ball. Be careful not to press the ball too flat.

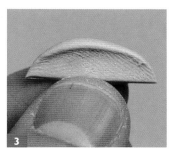

Step Three Using a utility knife, cut the excess clay away, leaving the section that will be used to form the lower lip.

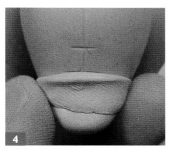

Step Four Holding the lip by the end that was cut and making sure not to distort the shape of the actual lip, line it up below the reference line you scored earlier.

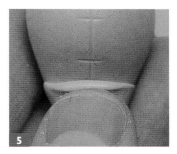

Step Five Attach the lip one side at a time. Using the side of your thumb, press the corners of the lips to the face and pull off the excess. By pulling off the excess instead of cutting, the lip will be easier to blend.

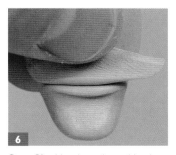

Step Six Use the stylus to blend in the bottom of the lip. Create the upper lip in the same way as you did the lower. Then holding it with the tip of your thumb, line it up with the lower lip.

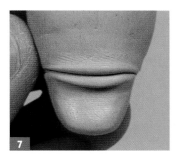

Step Seven Blend in the upper lip with the stylus. Keep in mind that the lower lip should be slightly larger and stick out farther than the upper lip.

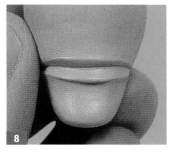

Step Eight Now you are ready to give the lips more form. Line up the bottom of the handle of a utility knife with the crease of the lips, and gently roll the handle from side to side.

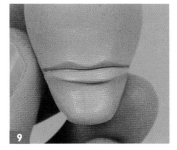

Step Nine Notice that the mouth has begun to flatten out. Now form the upper lip indentation. Using your pinky, lightly press the center of the upper lip.

Nose

When sculpting the nose, keep in mind that there are millions and millions of different noses—round, pointed, flat, flared, or even hooked. I'll give you basic techniques for sculpting noses, and you can experiment with different shapes and sizes.

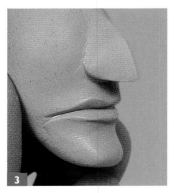

Step One Decide how large you want the nose to be, and start with a ball of clay slightly larger than that. Shape the clay into a pyramid. Keep the tip of the nose facing you and the back of the nose resting on the tip of your index finger.

Step Two As you rest the nose on your finger, use the tips of your thumbs to create the nostrils. Gently press in the corners of the nose, but don't press in too deeply. Remember: the operative word here is *gently*.

Step Three Align the nose with the grid you created earlier. Using the tip of a stylus, gently blend the clay from the nose into the face. As you blend, you can continue to add form to the sides of the nostrils with the side of a pair of tweezers.

Cheeks

As with the nose, there are many different shapes of cheeks and jowls. You can give your face high cheekbones and a lean and hungry look, or have them sagging and drooping.

Step One Begin with a ball of clay approximately 1/2" wide, and cut it in two. Each half will become one cheek. Holding the half-sphere between the thumb and index finger, shape the clay into an elongated triangle.

Step Two Line up the cheeks on each side just above the nostrils at the top and just below the corners of the mouth at the bottom. Use the stylus to blend the cheeks, but be careful not to damage the lips and nose.

Eyes and Eyelids

Using the tips of your pinkies, decide where you will place the eyes, and create indents on both sides of the face. Don't worry about making the indents too large or not having enough room left for a forehead. After the eyes are in, we'll build up the brow area.

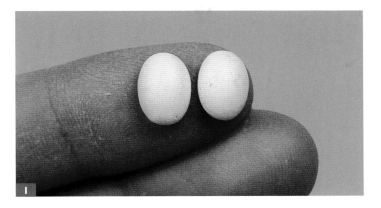

Step One For the eyeballs, roll a white ball slightly larger than 5/16" in diameter. Cut the ball into equal halves. Keeping the flat base of the half circle on the tip of your index finger, shape each eye into an oval. Next align both eyes in the indentations you've already formed on the face.

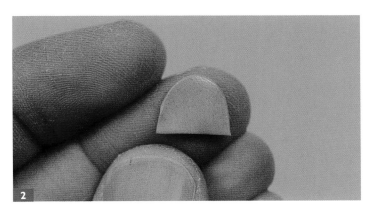

Step Two For the darker eyelids, mix a small amount of purple clay with the skin-colored clay used for the face, and knead well. Make a ball approximately 1/4" wide, and roll it into a small tube about 1/2" long. Flatten out the tube with your thumb, and then feed it through a pasta maker at the #5 setting. Measuring from the rounded ends of the flattened clay, cut both ends approximately 3/8" long.

Step Three Shape each piece into a curved lid by slightly pinching the rounded end. Starting from the corner of the eye closest to the nose, wrap the lid to the shape of the eye. Make sure to align both lids evenly.

Brow

Before actually attaching the eyebrow to the face, take the time to practice each step in this section several times. After a few tries, the brow should be easy to master.

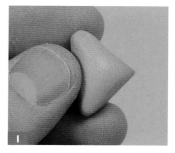

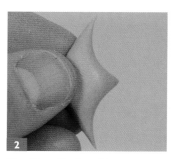

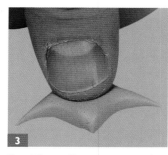

Step One Start with a ball approximately 5/8" in diameter. Using the thumb and index finger of both hands, pinch the clay into a triangular shape, so that one side is slightly longer than the other two sides.

Step Two Gently pull two corners of the clay. The center point of the shape will be placed above the bridge of the nose. The edges that have been pulled and extended will be wrapped around the outer sides of the eyes.

Step Three If you are not sure that the brow will fit, place it over the face to check the size. After sculpting the brow to the desired shape and size, create an indent just above the center portion of the brow with your finger.

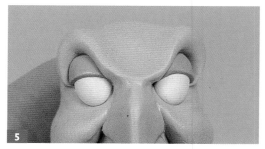

Step Four Cut off the excess clay just above the center portion of the brow. Align the base of the brow with the bridge of the nose. Attach by wrapping the ends of the brow around the corners of the eyes.

Step Five Use the stylus to blend the brow into the top of the head. To get an even blend, use the tip of your finger to smooth the clay. Your finger-prints will add an interesting skin texture to the face.

Irises

Where you position the irises on the eyeball determines the direction your sculpture's face looks—up, down, straight-forward, or cross-eyed.

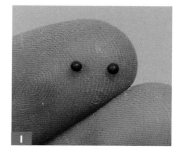

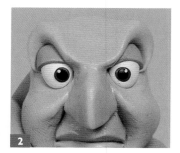

Step One For the irises, cut a blue ball approximately 1/16" wide into two equal halves. Roll each half into two smaller balls. Using the tip of a pair of tweezers or the flat end of a stylus, position each iris on the white of the eyes.

Step Two Before flattening the irises onto the eyes, make sure that they are positioned correctly. Next add the spot of black clay in the center of the iris for the pupil. Finally, to make the highlight, add a tiny dot of white clay into the corner of each iris.

Hair

Here I show a very simple way to make hair, but as you get more comfortable with the following steps, you'll want to experiment with different hairstyles. Photos from fashion magazines come in handy as references.

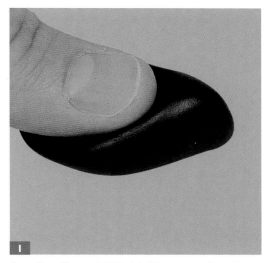

Step One Taper a 3/4" black ball into a cone shape. Press down the rounded end of the cone, and continue to push out the front section into a point. Cut off the excess clay in the back where you used your thumb to make the indent.

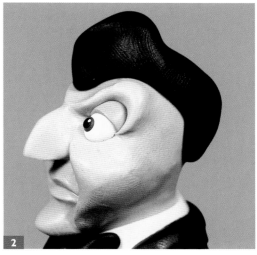

Step Two Position the hairpiece by placing the pompadour part of the hair on the center of the forehead. Blend the back of the hairpiece into the back of the head.

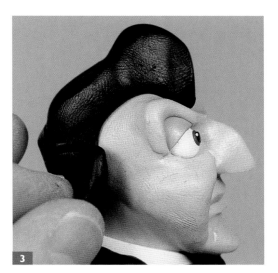

Step Three Cut a 3/4" black ball in two. Form each half into a ball and flatten. Starting on the sides of the head, wrap each piece around, and connect them in the back.

Step Four Keep blending and shaping the hair until you get the desired look. Roll the end of a utility knife handle through the hair to create individual strands.

15

Ears

To make sure that the ears are evenly aligned between the eyes and mouth, try this trick: Hold the face directly in front of you, and, using the tips of your index fingers, make small indentations on both sides of the head at the same time.

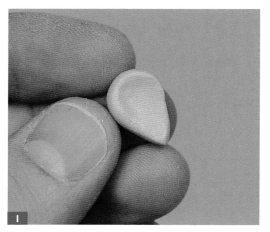

Step One Cut a 3/8" ball into two equal halves, and roll each half into two smaller balls. Using the same technique you used for the lips, lightly flatten one end of the ball, creating a ridged effect. Shape the rounded end into an ear, and cut off the excess.

Step Two Position the ear so that the top of the ear is even with the top of the eyes, attach, and blend. Using the tweezers' handle, create the detail inside the ears. (If you want a fuller hairstyle, make a few hair strands and partially cover the ears, blending the strands into the hairline.)

Eyebrows

Bushy or thin, arched or straight, eyebrows can be very expressive. It's best to make them the same color as the hair.

Step One Roll two small, equal-sized tubes roughly 1/2"–3/4" long. Taper the ends of each, making sure that one end of the eyebrow is slightly longer than the other.

Step Two To attach each eyebrow, position the shorter end above the bridge of the nose and wrap around the outer bridge of the eye.

Moustache

If you decide that you would like to add more detail, creating a moustache is one way to go. This is a simple moustache, but you can customize it any way you like.

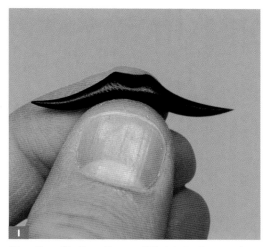

Step One Starting with a small black ball, roll out a tube roughly 3/8" long. Taper the ends of the tube, creating points at both ends. Indent the center so the moustache will fit snugly under the nose.

Step Two To attach the moustache, begin just underneath the nose. You can bend the ends of the moustache upward to create handlebars, spread them out across the cheeks, or taper the ends downward to make a Fu Manchu or goatee.

Facial Expressions

When sculpting faces, keep a mirror nearby. Look at your own face to see what happens to your eyes, eyebrows, forehead, cheeks, and mouth when you express various emotions.

One sure way to achieve a comical look is to give your sculpture crossed eyes, a big nose, and a bushy 'stache.

With his clenched jaw, wide eyes, and raised eyebrows, this "suit" could be saying, "Gotcha!"

It's unusual to model a face with closed eyes (probably why I did it!). Is he laughing or dreaming? You decide.

Hands

In animation, characters are drawn with three fingers instead of four because it's both easier and funnier. That's why I'll be demonstrating hands with three fingers and a thumb, but by all means, add another finger if you so choose.

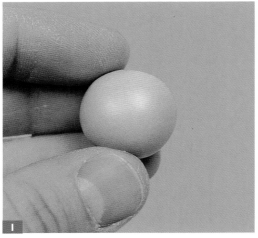

Step One Start by rolling out two equal-sized balls, each approximately 3/16" in diameter.

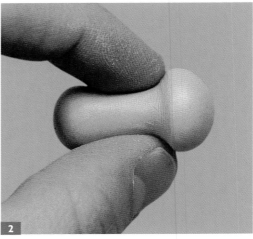

Step Two Holding the ball slightly off-center, gently roll it back and forth, creating a mushroom shape.

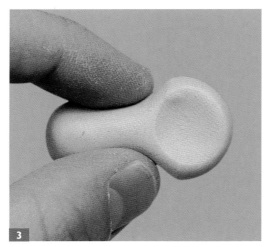

Step Three Lightly pinch the center of the mushroom shape, creating a paddle. The paddle will form the fingers and thumb, and the remaining section will form the wrist and arm.

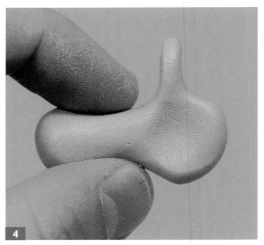

Step Four On one side of the paddle, pinch a small portion of the clay, and roll it out to form a thumb. (When sculpting the second hand, remember to put the thumb on the opposite side.)

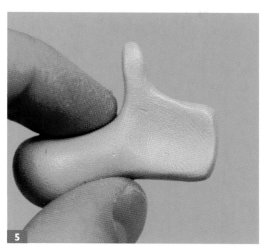

Step Five After you have smoothed and added definition to the thumb, square out the rest of the hand area. You want to keep this area thick enough to cut out the fingers, so don't pinch it too much.

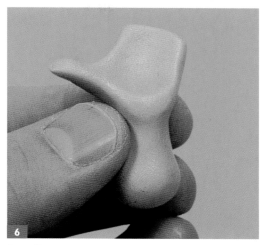

Step Six To shape the area of the palm and wrist, hold the hand between both of your index fingers and roll. As you gently turn the hand back and forth between your fingers, you'll notice that the wrist starts to take shape.

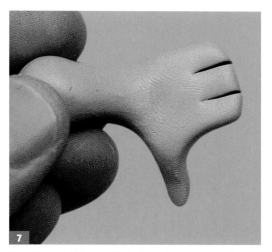

Step Seven Using a utility knife, make two cuts to form three fingers of equal size. Hold the hand by the arm, and carefully spread the fingers apart.

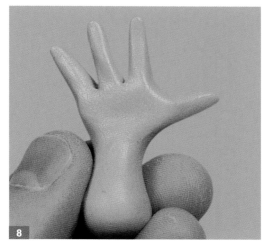

Step Eight Roll each finger back and forth between your thumb and index finger. Extend, taper, and smooth the end of each finger.

Shoes

From dress shoes to sneakers, flats to high heels, each type of shoe has its own look. These are black and white wingtips, but you can substitute other color combinations. Begin by rolling out a long sheet of black clay through the #6 setting of a pasta maker. Cut out two 1" squares and two 3/4" squares from the sheet of clay.

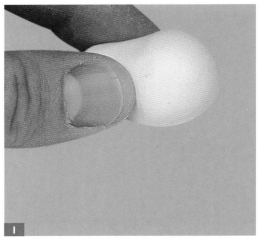

Step One Roll out two white balls approximately 1" in diameter. Using your thumb and index finger, press down a small section of the ball, creating the narrower back portion of the shoe.

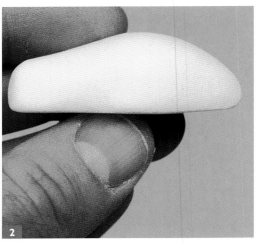

Step Two Shape the shoe so that the toe is somewhat pointed, the center is slightly higher than the rest, and the heel is elongated. Both left and right shoes should curve inward just a little.

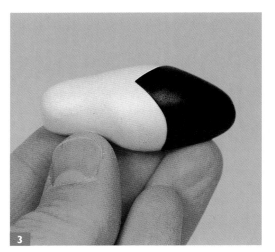

Step Three Take a square of black clay and place one of its corners about 1" from the tip of the shoe. Wrap the remaining corners around the front of the shoe, and trim away the excess from the base of the shoe.

Step Four Next you'll need two black triangles (made by cutting the 3/4" square along the diagonal). Attach one triangle on either side of the shoe directly in back of the black tip.

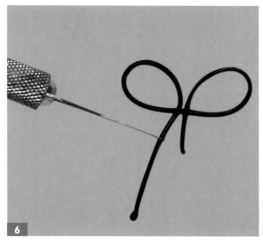

Step Five To make the sole, cut two strips about 1/4" x 1/8". Start at the back of the shoe, and wrap the strip around the shoe's base. Trim any excess and blend.

Step Six To make the shoelaces, roll out a very long, thin tube, and twist it into a bow or into a pretzel shape. Cut off the excess.

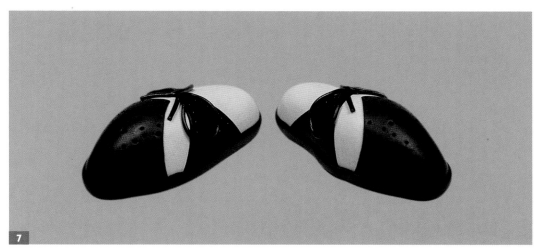

Step Seven Using a stylus, make the wingtip perforations in the black sections of the shoes. With the stylus tip, attach the shoelace bow in the center of the shoe where the triangles meet.

Pierre the Waiter

We're going to use the head, hands, and feet we created in Basic Sculpting Techniques (pages 10–17) for Pierre the Waiter. But don't attach the hair to the head just yet. This will make it easier to blend the head to the body.

You will need:

- white clay (2 packages)

- black clay (2 packages)

- skin-colored clay (custom-make your own using 2 packages of beige mixed with a little raw sienna)

- sandwich toothpick

- 1/8"-diameter wooden dowel at least 5" long

- tweezers or flat-tipped sculpting tool

- utility knife

- stylus

- glue

Step One For the body, start with a large ball of skin-colored clay that is free of air bubbles. Hold the clay in one hand, and with the thumb and index finger of your other hand, continuously turn the clay to create an hourglass shape. The length of the body should be roughly 3-1/4" from the bottom of the waist to the top of the neck. Extend the excess clay up through the neck, and then trim it off.

Step Two Insert a large sandwich toothpick straight down through the neck, leaving at least 1/2" sticking out. Place the head on the toothpick, and blend the neck into the head. For added strength, roll a small amount of clay into a thin tube, and wrap it around where the head and neck join. Blend gently and thoroughly.

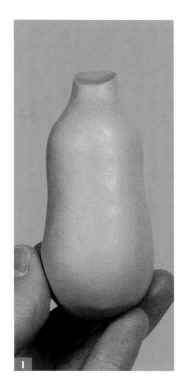

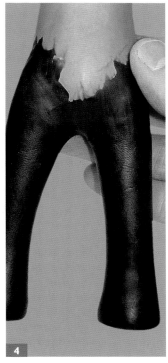

Step Three For the pant legs, roll out a black cylinder roughly 6" long by 1" wide, and cut it into two equal halves. Using your thumb, lightly press each cylinder down so it becomes slightly compacted. Starting in the middle, roll out the cylinder so that the middle is thinner than both ends.

Step Four Cut one end off both pant legs at an angle. Form a cup at the end that you just cut. Affix the pants legs to the body by attaching the cupped ends just below the waist and blend. Don't worry about the black clay looking messy. The top layers of clothing will cover it so it won't show.

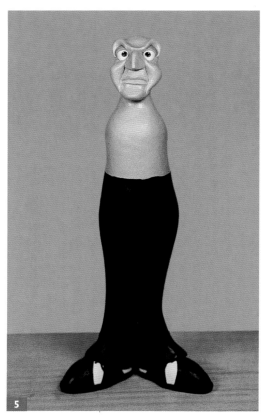

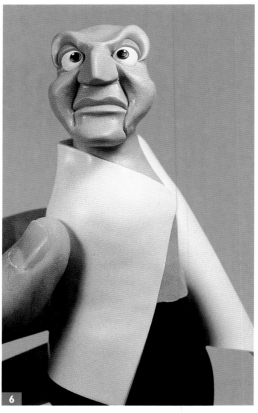

Step Five Flare out the bottom of the pant legs for a bell-bottomed look, and lightly press the pants over the shoes so the clay sticks. Do not blend. Then, with one hand holding the waist and the other the ankles, gently stretch the legs to elongate them. But don't stretch too much! Insert a 1/8" dowel through the base of the shoe up into the waist.

Step Six (Leave enough of the dowel sticking out at the base so the sculpture can be propped on a wood block when it's time for baking.) For the shirt, roll out a sheet of white clay at the #5 setting on the pasta maker. Beginning at the front of the body, just below the neck, wrap the clay sheet around the body as though it were a blanket.

Use these templates for Pierre's black jacket and lapels.

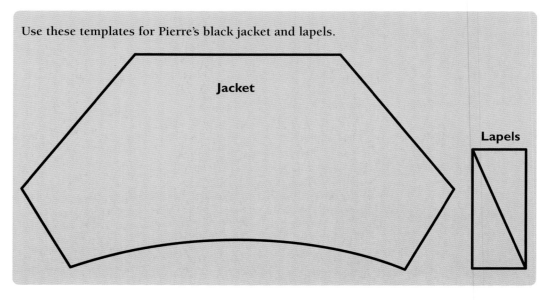

Jacket

Lapels

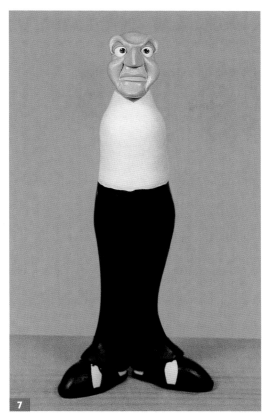

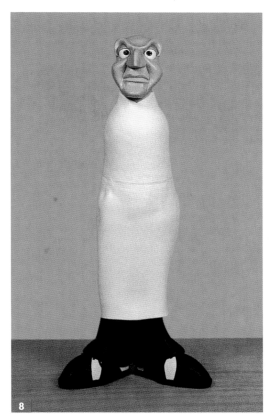

Step Seven Cut off the shirt excess, and blend the edges smooth. To make the apron, roll out a sheet of white clay at the #5 setting, and cut it into a 2-1/4" × 3" rectangle. Holding the clay sheet so that the 2-1/4" sides are on the top and bottom, gently stretch the clay.

Step Eight Gather one end of the 2-1/4" side of the apron sheet into pleats. Attach the apron around the front of the waist and blend. Don't attach the sheet too tightly or too close to the body—you want it to hang loosely and drape the way a real cloth apron would.

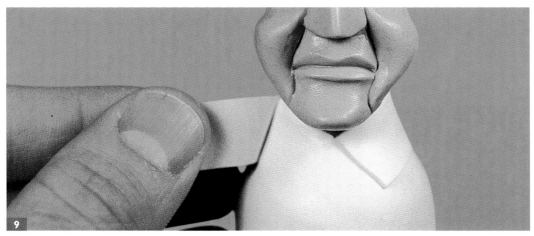

Step Nine For the shirt collar, cut a 3/8"-wide strip of white clay. Wrap the strip around the neck, placing it slightly above the top of the shirt. Cut the collar ends at an angle, as shown.

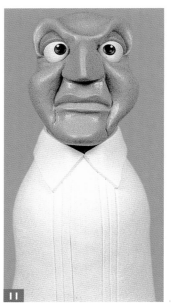

Step Ten Score the shirt collar with a utility knife, creating the look of a sewn seam. Remove the excess clay, and smooth out the edges.

Step Eleven Using a stylus, score lines down each side of the front of the tuxedo shirt to give the appearance of pleats.

Step Twelve Use the template on page 24 to cut out the jacket from a sheet of black clay, rolled out at the #5 setting. Starting at the belly, wrap the jacket around the body.

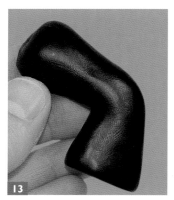

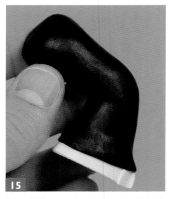

Step Thirteen Create the arms from a 5-1/2"-long black cylinder; cut in two (just as you did with the pant legs). Taper and bend them into position. Don't forget the elbow bulge!

Step Fourteen Attach a strip of white clay around the wrist area of the sleeve, creating a cuff where the ends meet. Blend the clay into the sleeve.

Step Fifteen Attach a strip of black clay just above the white strip and blend. This gives the appearance of the shirt cuff coming out of the sleeve of the jacket.

Step Sixteen Cup the ends of the arms, and attach them to the body at the shoulders. Before blending and smoothing the clay, make sure the arms are positioned exactly where you want them to be.

Step Seventeen Make the jacket collar the same way you did the shirt collar. Next, use the template on page 24 to cut out the lapels. Position them next to the collar and smooth.

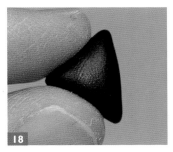

Step Eighteen For the bow tie, cut a 1/2" black ball in half, and roll into two smaller balls. Shape each half into a triangle with rounded corners. Gently press the two pieces together until they stick.

Step Nineteen Wrap a small piece of clay around the center of the bow tie where the two wings meet to create the knot. Use a flat-tipped sculpting tool to smooth out the knot and to score the four pleat lines.

Step Twenty With the same tool, press lightly to attach the bow tie and buttons. Make and attach the hair, eyebrows, and moustache using the techniques you've already learned (refer to pages 15–17).

Step Twenty-One Position the hands you made earlier (see pages 18–19) so you know they fit, but don't attach them securely. You will want to bake the sculpture and the hands separately since the hands will finish so much faster than the body. When baking, keep the sculpture propped up on the block of wood so the figure will stand up straight. After baking and cooling, glue on the hands (and any additional props you've devised, such as the wine bottle and the platter).

Fazzy Bunny

Now that you've learned to sculpt a human, it's time to move on to other subjects. Fazzy Bunny is a fairly easy critter to model, and one you can tailor to your own liking with different ears, clothing, and props.

You will need:

- white clay (2 packages)

- light blue clay (1 package, or mix your own with white and a little bit of blue)

- dark green clay (1 package)

- orange clay (1 package)

- black clay (just a little for the pupils)

- silver clay (just a little for the suspender clasps)

- pink clay (just a little for the nose)

- purple clay (just a little for the patch)

- bright green clay (just a little for the carrot top)

- sandwich toothpick

- tweezers

- utility knife

- stylus

- glue

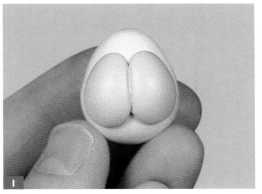

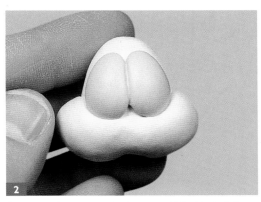

Step One For the head, roll out a 1" white ball. Form the ball into an egg shape. For the eyes, cut a 3/8" light blue ball into equal halves, and shape each half into semi-flattened egg shapes. Slice off a sliver from the inside of each eye so the two eyes lay flush against each other.

Step Two For the cheeks, shape two 3/4" white balls into egg shapes similar to the head. Using your thumb, press the thicker end of the egg shape to make a cup. Attach the cupped end of the cheeks to each side of the head. Make sure the cheeks lay flush just below the eye line and blend.

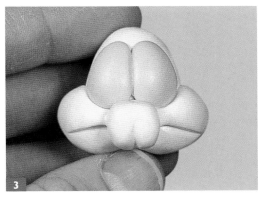

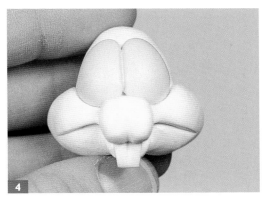

Step Three To form the muzzle, shape a 3/8" white ball into an egg shape. Cup the smaller end, and attach it just below the eyes. Using your thumb, slightly flatten the end and create a vertical crease down the middle. Make the cheek indentations with the end of the tweezers.

Step Four Using a 1/4" white ball, create the lower lip as you learned how to do in the lip technique section on page 11. Cut the shape of the teeth from a flattened strip of white clay, and attach so that it completely covers the lower lip.

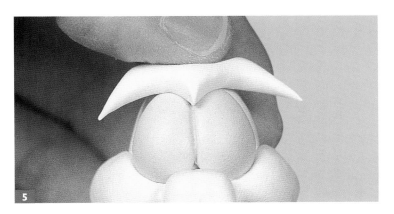

Step Five Create and attach the brow above the eyes. Fold down the sides, following the edges of the eyeballs. Blend the edges smooth with a stylus.

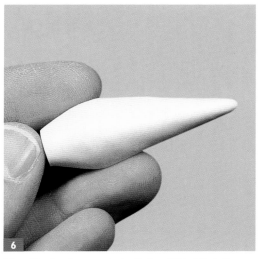

Step Six For the ears, start with two 3/4" white balls. Shape each ball into a cone shape, roughly 1-1/4" long.

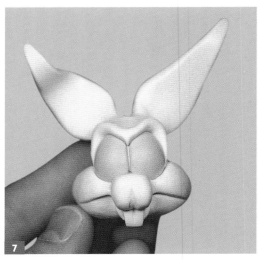

Step Seven Lay the ears on a flat surface, and lightly flatten one side. Then align them about 1/4" behind the eyes, attach, and bend into the desired positions.

Step Eight For the nose, shape a small pink ball into a triangle, and attach it to the end of the muzzle. Using a flat-tipped tool, like the end of tweezers, create the pupils of the eyes. Add tufts of hair to the top of the head.

Step Nine For Fazzy's torso, start with a 1-3/8" white ball. Shape it so there's a slight curve to the chest. Attach the body and the head with a toothpick, just as you did with Pierre the Waiter. Blend and smooth the joining.

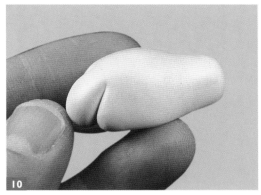

Step Ten For each foot, start with a white ball slightly smaller than 1". Shape it just as you would a shoe, but make toe indentations with the end of the tweezers.

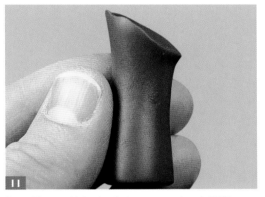

Step Eleven Make the dark green pant legs 1-1/4" long, cupping the ends that will attach to the torso.

Step Twelve Attach the legs to the torso. Then attach the feet to the legs, remembering to cup the ends of the pants.

Step Thirteen Form and attach the arms to the body. Add the overalls' bib section, pocket, and suspenders, crisscrossing the straps in back. If desired, add a patch to the knee of the pant leg and a tail to Fazzy's you-know-what. The more realistic and fine the details you add, the better!

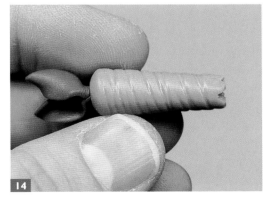

Step Fourteen For the carrot, roll out an orange tube, slightly tapering one end. Chop the tapered end for a "just chewed" look. For the leafy top, flatten three pieces of green clay into rounded diamond shapes and attach. Don't attach the carrot yet. After the sculpture has been baked and cooled off, you can glue the carrot into Fazzy's hand.

Chucky D. Beaver

You'll find that Chucky D. Beaver is very similar in construction to Fazzy Bunny. After you finish Chucky D., you might want to model a related animal: a mouse, squirrel, raccoon, prairie dog, or skunk, perhaps.

You will need:

- raw sienna clay
  (2 packages)

- blue clay (1 package)

- beige clay (1 package)

- white clay (1 package)

- black clay (1 package)

- silver clay (1 package)

- 2 dowels (each 1/8" in
  diameter and 2-1/2" long)

- 2 dowels (each 5/32" in
  diameter and 1" long)

- sandwich toothpick

- tweezers

- utility knife

- stylus

- glue

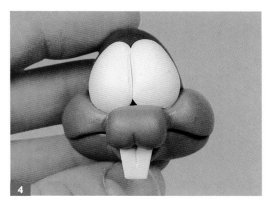

Step One For the head, start with a 1" sienna ball formed into an egg shape. For the eyes, cut a 3/8" white ball in half, and shape each into semi-flattened egg shapes. Cut a sliver from the inside of each eye so they'll fit flush together.

Step Two Mix equal parts raw sienna and beige clays for a lighter brown color. Shape two 3/4"-wide balls into egg shapes similar to the head. Using your thumb, press the thicker end of the egg shape to form a cupped indentation.

Step Three Attach the cheeks to each side of the head. Make sure the cheeks lay flush just below the eye line. Blend them together and smooth. Shape a 3/8" ball of the same color into an egg shape for the muzzle.

Step Four Attach the muzzle just below the eyes and flatten slightly. Using a 1/4" ball, create the lower lip. Cut the teeth from a flattened strip of white clay and attach. Use the tweezers' end to crease the muzzle, cheeks, and teeth.

Step Five Form and attach the eyelids, irises, and white highlights in the eyes. Then attach the eyebrow, and finish the face by adding the triangular black nose.

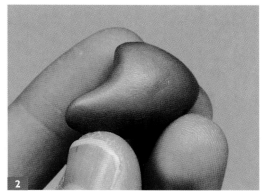

Step Six For the arm, begin with two equal-sized sienna tubes, 1-3/4" long. Taper and round out one end of the tube. Slightly flatten the rounded end.

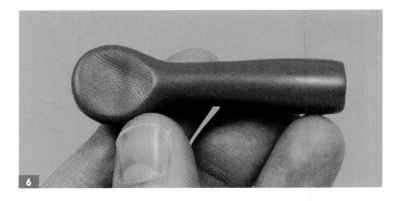

Step Seven Pinch a small amount of clay on one side of the flattened end to create a thumb. Make two cuts to form the three fingers.

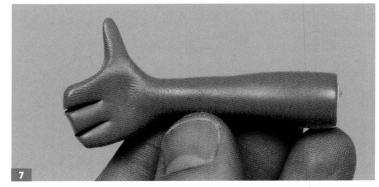

Step Eight Carefully spread the fingers apart. Taper the fingers (this will make them longer), and smooth the edges. After the arms have been sculpted, bend them into the desired poses.

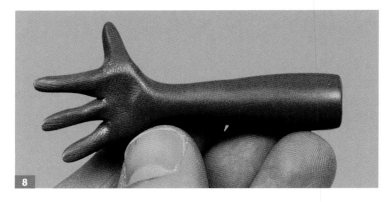

Step Nine To shape the hands for holding an object, use a dowel that is the same thickness as the object that will later be glued into the hand (in this case, 5/32" thick for both the hammer and the lunchbox handle). Wrap the fingers around the dowel. Leave the dowel attached during baking so the fingers don't move.

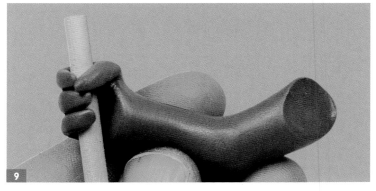

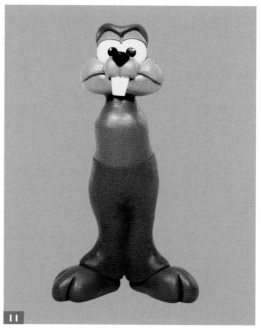

Step Ten Shape the body from a 1-1/2" ball of clay, slightly indenting Chucky D.'s waistline. Attach the head to the body with a round toothpick. Form and attach the blue pant legs just as you did with Pierre the Waiter and Fazzy Bunny.

Step Eleven Using 1" sienna balls, create the feet, and attach them to the pant legs, (Remember to cup and flare the leg bottoms when you do so.) Notice how the sculpture is at its widest at the waist and feet for stability.

Step Twelve Attach the arms to body. Remember to add the rounded shape of the shoulders. Without them, the arms will look as if they're sagging.

Step Thirteen Time to add some details: a strip of lighter brown clay for the chest; blue overalls bib, pocket, and suspenders; silver clasps; and a tuft of hair on his head.

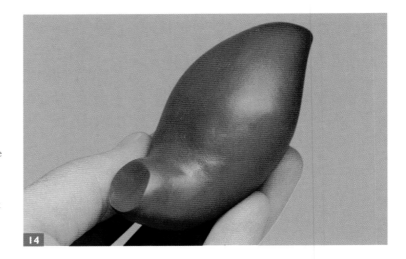

Step Fourteen For the tail, start with a 1-1/2" sienna ball, and roll it into a large cone shape. Taper both ends, but make one end much thinner than the other. Holding the tail between the palms of both hands, lightly flatten the tail. But don't flatten it too much—just enough to keep the rounded shape. Shape the tail into the desired pose.

Step Fifteen After the tail has been shaped to your liking, attach the lighter-colored brown clay sheet to the underside. Then, using the stylus, create the waffle grid detail that beavers have on the backs of their tails. You can place the tail on Chucky D.'s rear to see how it will look, but don't attach it yet. You want to bake the heavy tail separately from the main sculpture.

Step Sixteen For the lunchbox, roll out a 1" thick silver tube, and cut a piece 1-1/4" long. Keep one side of the tube round for the top, and flatten the other three sides to create the shape of the lunchbox.

Step Seventeen Add the hinge detailing to the front and back of the box as shown. When making the black handle, do not secure it tightly to the lunchbox. It will need to be removed so that it can be attached to Chucky's hand.

Step Eighteen For the hammer, make a 3/4" silver tube, and cut one end at an angle. Make a slit in the angled end for pliers and a groove for the head. Be sure to make the handle the same thickness as the dowel used to shape the hand.

Step Nineteen After baking and cooling, remove the dowel, and slide the lunchbox handle through the fingers. Glue the handle to the hand, and then glue the lunchbox to the handle. Don't forget to glue on the tail!

Igor the Laboratory Assistant

Monsters are some of my favorite characters to sculpt. Here's Igor as he carries a cranial offering to his evil scientist master. You might want to create a bevy of bewitched beauties—Frankenstein, the Mummy, the Creature from the Black Lagoon, the Invisible Man (gotcha!).

You will need:

- gray clay (3 packages of black and 3 of white to mix the gray)

- burnt umber clay (2 packages)

- ecru clay (1 package)

- black clay (1 package)

- beige clay (1 package)

- raw sienna clay (1 package)

- white clay (a little for the teeth)

- purple clay (a little for the eye)

- sandwich toothpick

- 1/8"-diameter wooden dowel about 4-1/2" long

- tweezers or flat-tipped sculpting tool

- utility knife

- stylus

- glue

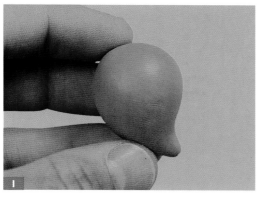

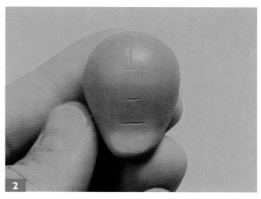

Step One To make the head, roll a gray ball approximately 1-1/8" wide. Taper the clay into an egg shape, and bend the smaller end outward to create the chin.

Step Two Draw a grid on the face to estimate the placement of eyes, nose, and mouth so you have something to line the features up to.

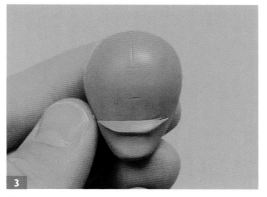

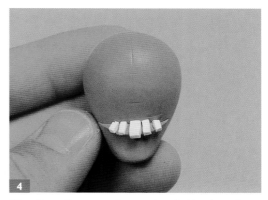

Step Three Form the lips using the technique demonstrated on page 11. Attach the lower lip first, but don't attach the upper lip until the teeth are in place.

Step Four Cut out small rectangles of white clay, and attach them unevenly across the lower lip for Igor's gap-toothed grimace.

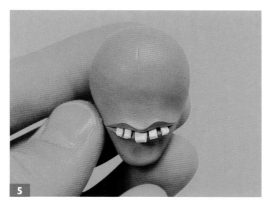

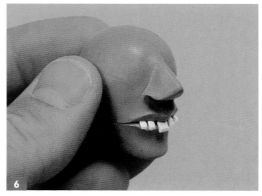

Step Five Attach the upper lip, and blend the edges with a stylus. Use your pinky to form the curving, center indentation of the lip.

Step Six As you learned earlier (see page 12), shape and attach the nose. No perfect, button nose for Igor—the more distorted you make his nose, the better!

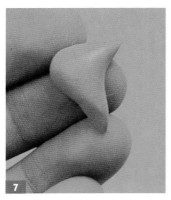

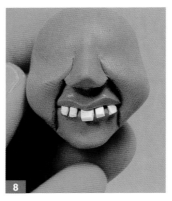

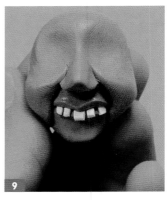

Step Seven For the cheeks, roll a ball of clay 1/2" wide, and cut it in two. Form both into triangular shapes.

Step Eight Line up the cheeks on each side of the mouth. Use the stylus to lightly blend them in.

Step Nine Pressing gently with both of your thumbs, make shallow indentations for the eyes.

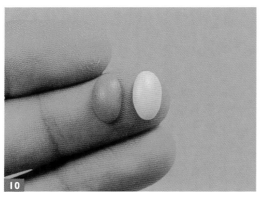

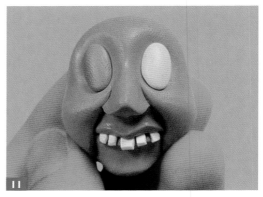

Step Ten For the eyeballs, roll out an ecru ball and a purple ball (both 5/16" wide). Cut them in half, and shape one half of each color into an oval with a flat base.

Step Eleven Align the two ovals in the indentations you've already prepared. The purple oval will be an eye that is swollen shut. Lovely!

Step Twelve With the stylus, form a "shut-eye" crease and wrinkles in the purple oval. For the other eye, follow the steps on pages 13–14 to create the purple eyelid and iris.

Step Thirteen Create and attach the brow above the eyes. Fold down the sides, following the edges of the eyeballs. Blend with a stylus, and add a few wrinkles.

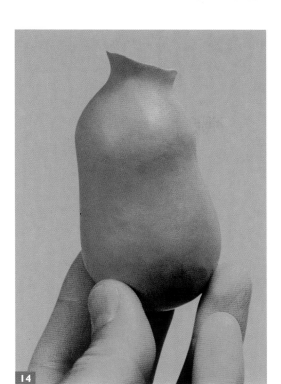

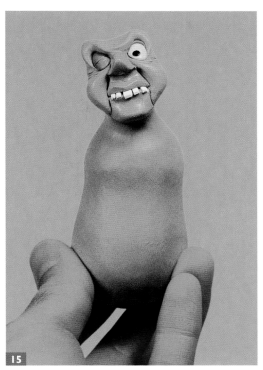

Step Fourteen For the body, start with a large ball of gray clay, and shape it into a lumpy, stocky torso approximately 3" long from top to bottom. Extend the excess clay up through the neck, and then trim it off.

Step Fifteen Attach the head to the body using a sandwich toothpick for stability. To add some "hunch" to Igor, attach the neck more toward the back of the head, and tilt the head slightly to the side.

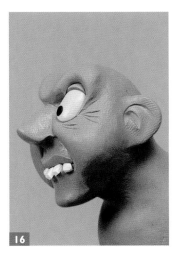

Step Sixteen Form and attach the ears. Again, keep in mind that two ears of different shape and size will only add to Igor's appeal.

Step Seventeen Sculpt and position the hands as shown. (You will bake them separately from the body, and attach with glue after they cool.)

Step Eighteen Position the hands one on top of the other so they are "cupped" and able to hold the proffered brain.

Step Nineteen Using raw sienna clay, sculpt and shape the shoes. To add a bit of "cartooniness," curl up the shoe tips.

Step Twenty Create the pant legs from a black clay cylinder cut in half. Cup the ends, attach the bottoms of the pant legs to the shoes, and attach the tops to the body. Insert a 1/8"-diameter wooden dowel through one of Igor's legs, and prop the sculpture on a block of wood.

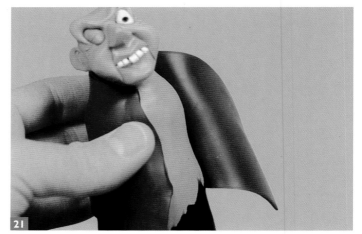

Step Twenty-One Using burnt umber clay, roll a sheet through the #4 setting of the pasta maker. Wrap a small sheet of clay around the top of the body.

Step Twenty-Two Trim the excess off just above the waist.

Step Twenty-Three Roll another sheet of burnt umber through the #1 setting of the pasta maker, and wrap it around the bottom of the body. Blend the areas where the two sections meet. Using ecru clay, roll out a thin rope approximately 1/8" thick. Wrap the rope around the waist, creating a knot in the front of the cloak.

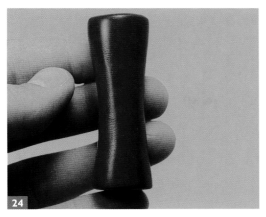

Step Twenty-Four Create the arms from a burnt umber clay cylinder cut in two (just as you formed the pant legs).

Step Twenty-Five Bend the arms at right angles, and give a little bulge to the elbow area.

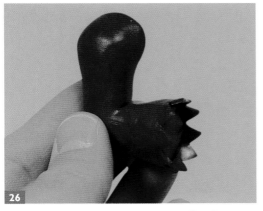

Step Twenty-Six To make the tattered cuffs, roll out a clay sheet using the pasta maker's #4 setting. Cut two strips 1/2" wide and just long enough to wrap around the wrist. Cut out small triangles for a "ripped" look. Then wrap the piece of clay around the wrist area of the sleeve and blend.

Step Twenty-Seven Cup the ends of the arms, and attach them to the body at the shoulders. Give Igor a little extra clay in the shoulder department—he's built like a linebacker. Be sure the arms are positioned where you want them before you blend and smooth.

Step Twenty-Eight For the hair, use bristles from an old hairbrush, and place them throughout the top of the head at different angles.

Step Twenty-Nine For the brain, roll a beige ball about 1/2" wide, and flatten one side. Create the center crease and fissures with a stylus.

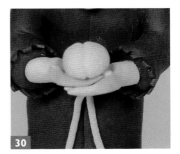

Step Thirty Bake the body, hands, and brain. After the sculpture has cooled off, glue the hands to the arms and the brain to the hands.

Rupert the Dragon

Who says you have to limit yourself to real animals and real objects? Try your hand at sculpting fantasy creatures and let your imagination go wild!

You will need:

- turquoise clay (6 packages)
- white clay (1 package)
- gold clay (1 package)
- black clay (just a little)
- dark blue clay (just a little for the eyelids, or you can mix your own using turquoise and black)
- sandwich toothpick
- silver pen to paint the toothpick sword
- Balsa Foam™
- black and gray acrylic paints (other colors as desired)
- old paintbrush and old toothbrush
- tweezers
- utility knife
- stylus
- glue

Step One For the head, use a 3/4" turquoise ball, and cut 1/4" off the end. Make the white eyes using the same amount of clay you cut from the head.

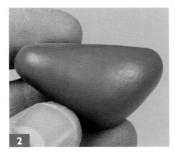

Step Two For the muzzle, use about 1-1/2 times the clay that you used to make the head. Round it into the triangular shape you see here.

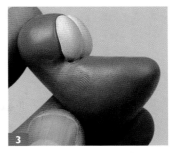

Step Three Cut the end of the muzzle at an angle, and indent to form a cup. Fit the head into the cupped end to attach.

Step Four Form the lips using the technique on page 11. Attach the upper lip first, and then add the lower lip. Using the end of a utility knife handle, add definition to the lips.

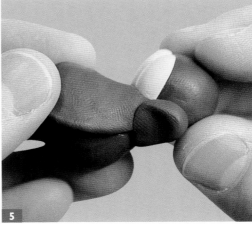

Step Five For the cheeks, cut a 3/8" ball in two. Flatten one side of each half, and attach at the corner of the mouth just below the eye. Indent with your thumb.

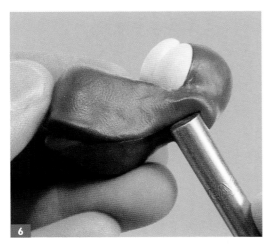

Step Six To make the crease in the cheeks, roll the end of a utility knife along the center lip line. Roll upward to create a grin, or roll downward to create a sneer.

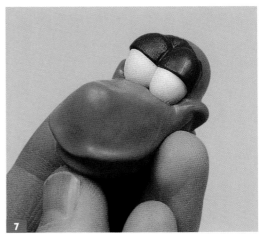

Step Seven Make the eyelids with dark blue clay. (If you need to, you can refer back to page 13.) Attach each lid to cover half of the eyeball. Blend the edges.

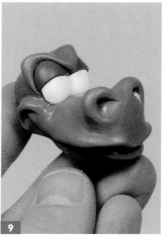

Step Eight Make the eyebrow, attach it above the eyes, and then blend the sides around the corners of the eyes.

Step Nine For the nostrils, cut a ball in two, and attach each half on either side of the muzzle. Indent both with the end of a utility knife.

Step Ten Using the tip of the tweezers, attach the dots that make up the iris and pupil. Don't forget the white highlight.

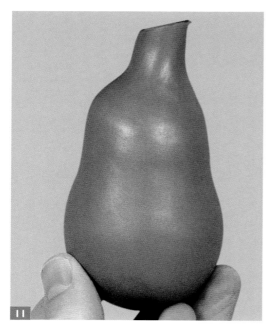

Step Eleven From a 3-1/2" ball of clay, sculpt the body into a bottom-heavy pear shape. Insert a 1/8" wood dowel into the neck to support the weight of Rupert's large head.

Step Twelve Place the head onto the protruding end of the wood dowel to attach it to the body. Blend the neck until it's smooth.

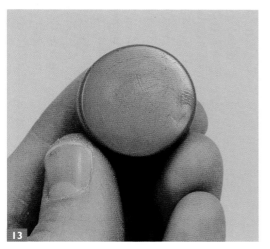

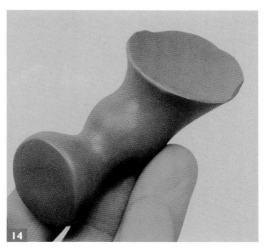

Step Thirteen For the hands and feet (which are the same size and shape), cut two 1" balls in half, and smooth the flat side on all four pieces.

Step Fourteen Cut a 4" tube in half. Shape the legs, leaving one end bulky and the other end tapered. Cup the tapered ends, attach the feet, and then bend as desired.

Step Fifteen Attach the legs to the body, cupping the ends and blending. Position them as you like. Follow the same steps for making and attaching the arms as for the legs. Make and attach the arms following the same steps you used for the legs.

Step Sixteen For the nails, roll out eight 1/2" white balls. Using the index finger and thumb of both hands, press down on both sides of each ball, creating pyramid shapes. Cut the pyramids in two. (Each half is a nail.)

Step Seventeen On each hand, attach three nails so they butt up against each other. The thumbnail should be spaced a little farther away. Attach three toenails on each foot.

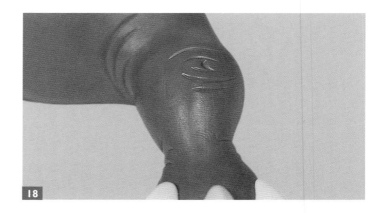

Step Eighteen Using the back of a pair of tweezers or a flat-headed sculpting tool, add creases to give a wrinkled look to the knees. You might also want to incise crease lines on the elbows and shoulders.

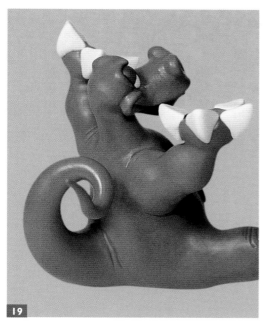

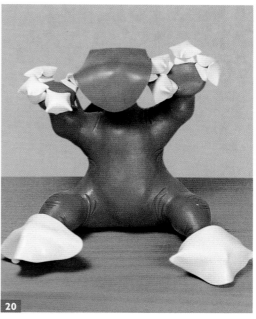

Step Nineteen For the tail, roll out a 1-1/2" turquoise tube, tapering the end to a long point. Cup the wider end, and attach it to the bottom of the dragon. Blend, smooth, and twist the tail into a fanciful curlicue.

Step Twenty Prepare the sculpture for baking, keeping in mind that thinner areas will bake faster than thicker areas. To prevent burning, cover the head, tail, hands, and feet with thin sheets of clay.

Step Twenty-One Props such as this sword (gold Premo for the handle and a large toothpick colored with a silver pen for the blade) can lend a storytelling dimension to your sculpture: "After finishing a meal of errant knight (flambéd, of course), Rupert the Dragon uses the knight's sword as a toothpick."

Cobblestone Base

Here's how to make a realistic-looking rock or cobblestone base for Rupert (or any of your sculptures) out of Balsa Foam™, a product that's available at most hobby and craft stores.

Step One Start with a square of 1/2" thick Balsa Foam™ that's big enough for your sculpture to rest on. Lightly score the irregular stone shapes with a stylus or any sharp tool.

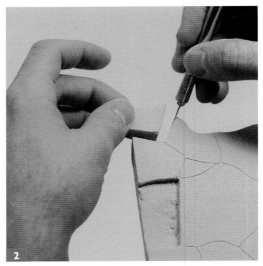

Step Two File down a few of the cobblestones to add depth. For added interest, cut away some of the shapes around the edges with a utility knife.

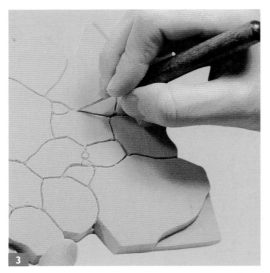

Step Three With a stylus, carve the cobblestone outlines a little more deeply. Add a few more dents and pits while you're at it.

Step Four Using either your fingertips or very fine grit sandpaper, rub along the outline of each stone and the sides of the base to round their edges.

Step Five Paint the base with black acrylic paint diluted with warm water. Use an old brush because you want to really mash the paint into the cracks and crevasses.

Step Six After the black acrylic paint has dried (about 5 minutes), go over it lightly with gray that you've thinned with water. The black undercoat will show through the gray wash.

Step Seven Use an old, throwaway toothbrush to add flecks of color. Using just a little paint at a time, dab the bristles in the paint, and flick them with your thumb.

Step Eight To give the cobblestones a gritty look with realistic highlights, speckle them with different acrylic paint colors: purple, light blue, yellow, and white.

Wendell the Rhino

Winsome Wendell is shown here *au naturel,* as most rhinos are happy to be. Here are some other similar projects that you might try: a hippo in a toga, an elephant in a grass skirt, or a stegasaurus in a loincloth.

You will need:

- white clay (4 packages)

- black clay (4 packages)

- purple clay (just a little for the eyelids)

- sandwich toothpick

- 1/8"-diameter dowel (approximately 3" long)

- tweezers

- utility knife

- stylus

- glue

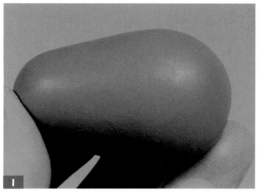

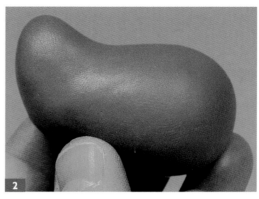

Step One Mix equal amounts of black and white clay to make gray. Wendell's head is made in the same way you made Rupert the Dragon's in the previous project. Gently roll the muzzle to create a smooth tapered shape.

Step Two For the back portion of the head, cut a 3/4" ball in half. Flaring out the ends of one of the halves, attach it to the top of the tapered end of the muzzle. Blend and smooth.

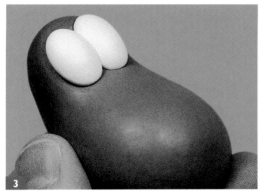

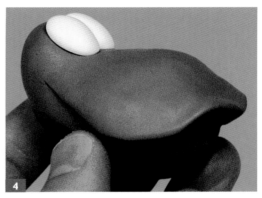

Step Three Using your pinky, create two indents in the head area for the eyes to set into, and attach the white eyes. Remember when fitting the eyes together to cut a sliver from each eye where they connect.

Step Four Score a line where the center of the lips will be; then create and attach the upper lip. Do the same for the bottom lip.

Step Five With the end of a utility knife, create the definition of the lips. Using the tip of your pinky, create the center indentation on the upper lip.

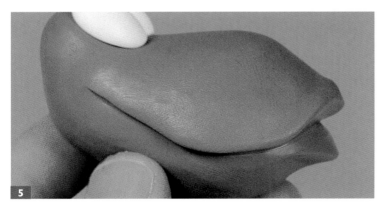

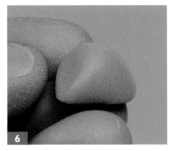

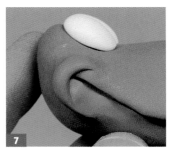

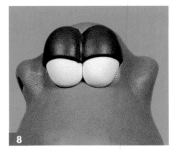

Step Six For the cheeks, cut a 3/8" ball in half. Flatten one side of the half-ball, and attach it just below the eye with the flat side facing the muzzle. Repeat for the other cheek.

Step Seven Using the end of a utility knife, press down to create the crease in each cheek for Wendell's goofy grin.

Step Eight Create the eyelids color by mixing a bit of purple with the gray. Attach the eyelids from the center to the sides, blending the corners and top.

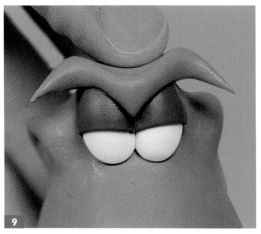

Step Nine Form the eyebrow. Then holding the brow by the tip of your thumb, attach it to the top of the eyes. Blend the flared ends around the corners of the eyes.

Step Ten To form the nostrils, cut a 3/8" ball in half. Flare the ends, and attach both on either side of the muzzle. Use the end of a utility knife to make the indentations.

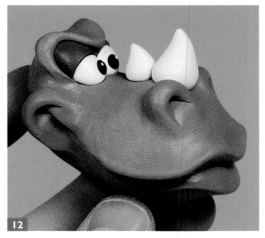

Step Eleven Using the back of a pair of tweezers or a flat-tipped sculpting tool, add the dots for the pupils, irises, and the important white highlights.

Step Twelve Attach two small horns to the top of the muzzle. (You can omit the horns to turn Wendell into a hippopotamus.)

Step Thirteen Shape and smooth the body from a 3-1/2" ball of clay. There are no waist, shoulder, and hip curves for this rotund rhino's body.

Step Fourteen Cup the tapered neck end of the body, and attach the head. Keep the back of the head flush with the back of the neck. Set aside while you form the limbs.

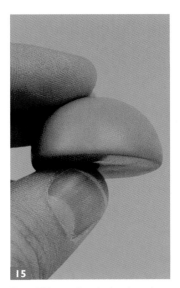

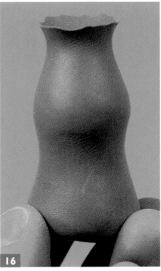

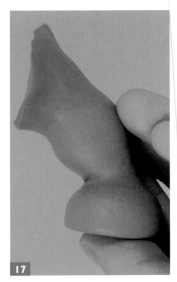

Step Fifteen For the hands and feet, cut two 1-1/8" balls in half. Smooth out the flat sides of the all four pieces.

Step Sixteen For the arms and legs, roll out two tubes, 3" long by 1" wide. Cut each tube in half, and sculpt a curvaceous hourglass for the limbs.

Step Seventeen Attach the hands and feet to the tapered ends of the arms and legs. Blend and position them as desired.

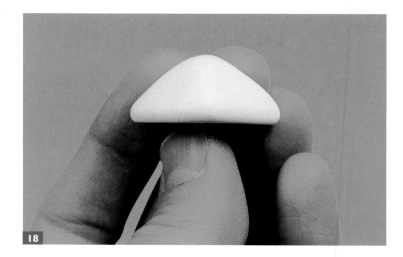

Step Eighteen For the six toenails, use three 5/8" white balls. Using the thumb and index finger of each hand, press the ball into a pyramid shape as shown here. Cut each pyramid into two equal triangular pieces.

18

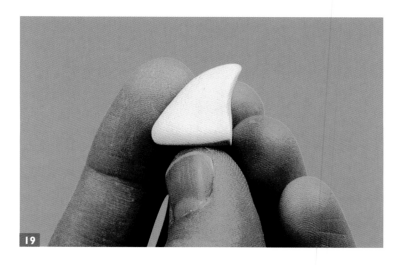

Step Nineteen For the eight fingernails, use four 1/2" balls, and follow the same steps as for the toenails. Attach the nails to the hands and feet.

19

Step Twenty Attach the arms and legs to the body. Make sure to cup the ends of the arms and legs to assure a better fit. Blend and smooth the connection. Add wrinkles and crease detailing to the body. If you want, shape a separate tail, and glue it on after baking.

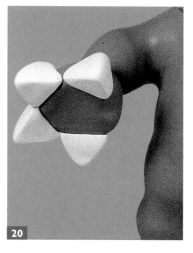

20

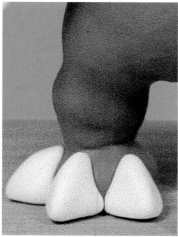

Gladiator Wendell

Wendell goes Roman with the addition of a glorious gladiator costume, proving that clothes really do make the rhino.

You will need:

- gold clay (3 packages)
- red clay (1 package)
- ecru clay (1 package)
- raw sienna clay (1 package)
- silver clay (1 package)
- tweezers
- utility knife
- stylus
- glue

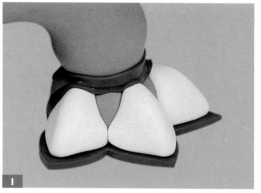

Step One Roll out a sheet of raw sienna clay using the #1 setting on a pasta maker. Cut four 6" strips. Starting at the base of each foot, wrap one strip from outside toe to inside toe. Wrap a second strip around the ankle. For the sandal sole, place the foot on the clay sheet, and cut around it.

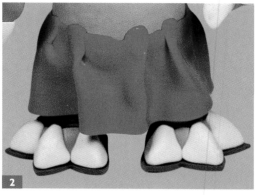

Step Two Using the #5 setting of a pasta maker, roll out a large sheet of red clay. Cut the sheet of clay so that it is roughly 1-3/4" wide. Wrap the clay around the body, gathering and pleating it as you go. Make sure that the skirt is not too long—you don't want to hide the sandals.

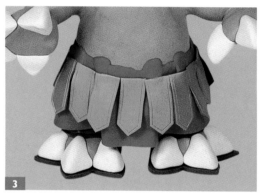

Step Three With the #1 setting, roll out a sheet of gold. Using template A, cut out 16 skirt shields, and attach them to the bottom of the skirt, with each one touching the next. Blend the straight ends of the shields so they are flush with the body. Add designs to the skirt panels with a stylus.

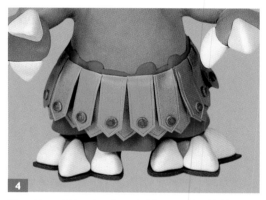

Step Four Cut out and attach 16 more skirt shields. Position this layer of shields so that the tip of the shield lies between two shields on the bottom layer. To add extra detail, place a circle of silver clay with a small dot of red clay in the middle, at the tip of each shield.

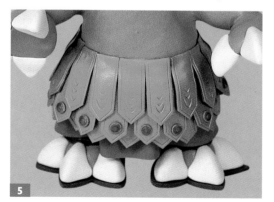

Step Five Cut out 16 more skirt shields, positioning each one so that the tips of the shields lie in between the shields on the last layer. Use the stylus to make a design on each panel. Be sure to blend the ends into the body at the waist.

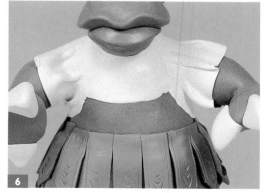

Step Six Roll out a large sheet of white clay through the #5 setting of a pasta maker. Wrap a piece around the neck, creating an undershirt. Using the same pleating method as for making the skirt, attach the sleeves.

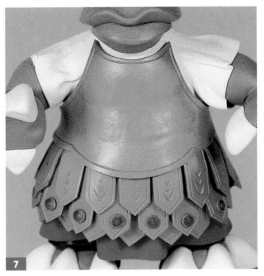

Step Seven Using the #1 setting of a pasta maker, roll out a sheet of gold clay. Cut out the breastplate and backplate, using template B as your guide. Attach the breastplate so that the white undershirt is visible at the neck and the bottom covers the top portions of the skirt shields. Trim the sides just under the arms. Repeat with the backplate. Connect both pieces under the arms, and smooth out.

Step Eight From a sheet of red clay, cut out 6 shoulder shields (template C), and attach three at the top of each shoulder, covering the shirtsleeve. Using gold clay, cut out two shoulder shields (template D) and position so that the ends overlap the breastplate and the backplate. Add rivets, bolts, and bow ties. Do the same for the backside of the armor. Score details into the front breastplate with a stylus.

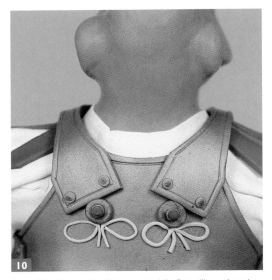

Step Nine To create the two armor plates that hold the front and back armor together, roll out a small sheet of gold clay at the #5 setting of a pasta maker. Cut two small rectangles, and attach just under the arms. Add small gold rivets in the corners. It's all in the details!

Step Ten The back of the head, while flat, still needs to be cut off before attaching the helmet. Start just above the eyelids, and slice downward at an angle. You may want to hold the back of the head steady with one hand as you cut. Then bake the rhino with its smaller parts covered with clay sheets.

Step Eleven Cut the helmet pieces from a gold clay sheet rolled through a pasta maker at the #1 setting. Then cut a 1-1/4" ball in two. Shape one half into an oval. Attach the neck shield (template E) and blend.

Step Twelve Cut out two ear shields (using template F as a guide), and attach to both sides of the helmet. Position the flaps so the straight side of the ear shield faces the front of the helmet.

Step Thirteen Position the helmet on Wendell's head, and gently curve the ear shields to follow the contours of the face. You will be taking it off later to bake separately.

Step Fourteen Score details in the face shield (cut from template G), and attach to the front of the helmet. Position so that it ends on the sides just behind the ear shields.

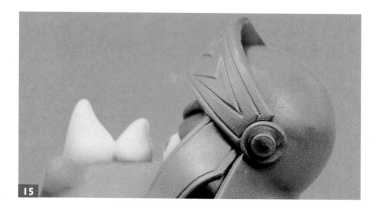

Step Fifteen Using two circles of clay (one large and one small), create the face shield hinge. Place one on either side, overlapping the ends of the face shield.

Copy my templates onto heavier card stock to use as patterns for the gladiator outfit.

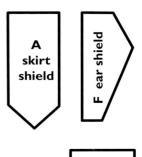

A
skirt
shield

F ear shield

Step Sixteen To create the plume on the top of the helmet, start with a 2" red clay circle that is approximately 1/2" thick.

Step Seventeen Cut a wedge from the circle; then trim the ends as shown. Using a stylus, incise "feather" lines. Bake the helmet and the plume.

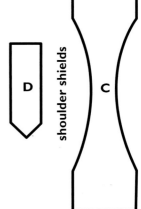

D

shoulder shields

C

Step Eighteen After the helmet and plume have cooled, roll a large ball of gold clay and place on top of the helmet. Push the plume into the ball of clay and leave for 5 minutes.

Step Nineteen Cut around the plume, creating a rectangular block. Remove the plume and rebake. After cooling, glue the plume in place, and then glue the helmet to the head.

E
neck shield

G   face shield

B
breastplate and backplate

61

And More. . .

Here's a gallery of just a few of my polymer clay sculptures. I love to find the details that are authentic, imaginative, mind-boggling, or just plain fun to create. The possibilities are endless.

Don't limit yourself to sculpting creatures and characters—any subject is fair game. This Bolex film camera looks more difficult to create than it really was. The legs are made from painted dowels and toothpicks.

The design of my knight series came from 15th-century German armor that I studied during a visit to the Metropolitan Museum in New York.

The chef series was inspired by my love for all types of cuisine from all around the world.

I built the piano for my concert pianist out of basswood, using actual piano blueprints from Steinway (reduced greatly, of course)!

I carry my sketchbook everywhere. This character is based on a drawing I did of a violinist at a summer concert at the Hollywood Bowl.

The title of this chess set for Warner Bros. is "Pirates of the Carrotbean." The chessboard is a treasure map in the shape of Bugs Bunny's head.

Each chess piece is based on a cartoon character, such as this closeup of a swash-buckling Pepe Le Pew.

This large piece commissioned for Warner Bros. is 20" x 15" (and 12" tall). Its name? "Ben Hare."

With precise execution, close attention to detail, and imagination, modeling with polymer clay can be taken to the professional, fine-art level. Indeed many of my sculptures are shown in art galleries and are commissioned and collected as fine art. There are so many possibilites for polymer clay modeling, I certainly hope you have as much creative fun with it as I do.